Sulfur

T0017210

Elise Tobler

Enslow Publishing
101 W. 23rd Street
Suite 240
New York, NY 10011
USA

enslow.com

Published in 2019 by Enslow Publishing, LLC.
101 W. 23rd Street, Suite 240, New York, NY 10011

Library of Congress Cataloging-in-Publication Data

Names: Tobler, Elise, author.
Title: Sulfur / Elise Tobler.
Description: New York : Enslow Publishing, [2019] | Series: Exploring the elements | Audience: Grades 5 to 8. | Includes bibliographical references and index.
Identifiers: LCCN 2018010170| ISBN 9781978503717 (library bound) | ISBN 9781978505469 (paperback)
Subjects: LCSH: Sulfur—Juvenile literature. | Periodic table of the elements—Juvenile literature.
Classification: LCC QD181.S1 T77 2018 | DDC 546/.723—dc23
LC record available at https://lccn.loc.gov/2018010170

Printed in the United States of America

To Our Readers: We have done our best to make sure all website addresses in this book were active and appropriate when we went to press. However, the author and the publisher have no control over and assume no liability for the material available on those websites or on any websites they may link to. Any comments or suggestions can be sent by email to customerservice@enslow.com.

Photo Credits: Cover, p. 1 (chemical element symbols) Jason Winter/Shutterstock.com; cover, p. 1 (sulfur mine) Karn Samanvorawong/Shutterstock.com; p. 8 Melnikov Sergey/ Shutterstock.com; p. 10 fzd.it/ Shutterstock.com; p. 11 Inna Bigun/ Shutterstock.com; p. 13 BlueRingMedia/ Shutterstock.com; p. 14 Images & Volcans/Science Source; p. 17 pupunkkop/ Shutterstock.com; p. 21 concept w/ Shutterstock.com; p. 23 vchal/ Shutterstock.com; p. 26 Bacsica/ Shutterstock.com; p. 28 Ungnoi Lookjeab/ Shutterstock. com; p. 31 Tony Freeman/Science Source; p. 34 Evannovostro/ Shutterstock.com; p. 35 bubblea/ Shutterstock.com; p. 37 Sadovnikova Olga/ Shutterstock.com; p. 40 Eva Mont/ Shutterstock.com; p. 41 NASA/Science Photo Library/Getty Images; p. 42 SIAATH/ Shutterstock.com.

Contents

Introduction

~~~~~~

Chemical elements make up everything in the world, everything in the *universe*. An element is a special kind of substance that contains only one kind of atom and cannot be made into a simpler form. Water is not an element even though it's made *of* elements; water is a compound of hydrogen and oxygen and can be broken down into its parts. To date, 118 elements have been discovered or created; 94 of these occur naturally, the other 24 have been synthetically created. Sulfur has been known to mankind since antiquity; the element had a variety of uses in Egypt, Greece, and China, from the fumigation of buildings in an effort to root out pests and diseases, to the treatment of certain skin conditions.

In the earliest days of alchemy, sulfur, along with mercury and salt, were believed to be a component of all metals. Indian alchemists called sulfur "the smelly," and many Biblical passages refer to the underworld smelling of brimstone, another word for sulfur. It's likely this pairing came from the smell of volcanoes; volcanic gas is rich in sulfur, whether it be sulfur dioxide or hydrogen sulfate.

Sulfur can be found in countless places on the earth: it's in the tires of your bicycle; it's in the food you eat; it's in matches, and was probably used to bleach the paper sitting in your printer. Hydrothermal vents, underwater cracks in the earth's crust, expel sulfur, as do hot springs. Without sulfur, most living things—including humans!—wouldn't be able to survive.

Sulfur is also found in the universe at large, within the hearts of some of the universe's largest stars and inside meteorites. Jupiter's innermost moon, Io, is heavily sulfuric, with over four hundred active volcanoes. Io also gets its orange and yellow coloring from sulfur allotropes and compounds of sulfur. Sulfur in the form of sulfur dioxide-frost also exists on the distant moon. On Io, plumes of sulfur and sulfur dioxide can reach up to 300 miles (500km) above the moon's surface—so imagine how smelly that moon would be!

And yet, sulfur in its purest form doesn't smell at all. It's sulfur compounds that carry a bad odor. Mercaptans are why defensive sprays from skunks smell so bad; hydrogen sulfide is why rotten eggs reek, and why stink bombs stink.

Sulfur also plays a role in our food industry, from the protection of agricultural crops to the preservation of some foods. In dried fruits, sulfur helps preserve the color and appearance of the fruit. In wine production, sulfur dioxide is valued as an antioxidant and antibacterial—it helps keep wine fresh.

Despite their great value, sulfur-containing substances may pose a hazard to both humans and the environment, so must be used with care and consideration. When burned, sulfur dioxide gas is produced, which presents itself as a common pollutant in the air, and a biproduct of making the gasoline your car runs on. Sulfur dioxide is also a common element of acid rain, so while it might preserve your wine, it's not good if it should rain onto your vineyard or other crops.

In this book, we'll take a look at how sulfur was discovered, how it helped form the world we know today, and where it may take us in the future.

1

Historically Speaking

Sulfur, identified by the chemical symbol S, is the seventeenth most abundant element on the earth. In its most common elemental form, sulfur is a bright yellow, crumbly substance that belongs to a category of elements known as the nonmetals. As a nonmetal, sulfur is a poor conductor of electricity and heat. Sulfur does not dissolve in water, but it does dissolve in certain organic solvents, such as carbon disulfide, benzene, and toluene

The name *sulfur* probably comes from the Sanskrit *sulvere,* the Latin *sulfurium,* or the Arabic *sufra*, all of which mean "yellow." While many people associate sulfur with the smell of rotten eggs, pure sulfur actually has no odor or taste. Only in its compound forms does sulfur smell.

In Indonesia, miners haul sulfur from volcanoes, making for dirty work—but sulfur in its pure form doesn't smell at all.

Archaeological Sulfur

Sulfur was known to humans long before the field of chemistry developed. In prehistoric times, a reddish-brown sulfur-containing pigment called cinnabar was used in cave paintings and other art forms. Archeological evidence also shows that prehistoric humans may have taken sulfur pills to relieve digestive problems.

Ancient Egyptians burned sulfur to produce fumes used to bleach their cotton. In the eighth century BCE, the Greek poet Homer referred to sulfur in the *Odyssey* when Odysseus requests sulfur so he may burn it and "purify the house." This is one of the oldest references to the use of sulfur dioxide as a fumigant, a gas that can kill vermin and possibly disease.

In some translations of the Bible, sulfur is referred to as brimstone, which, along with fire, destroyed the cities of Sodom and Gomorrah. During the Byzantine Empire, a fiery substance hurled at enemy ships probably contained sulfur, though the recipe for this "Greek fire" has been lost. In tenth-century China, the first recipe for gunpowder called for sulfur, still a component of explosives today.

Elementally Speaking

Despite its varied and widespread use throughout history, sulfur did not reveal its true chemical identity until the late 1700s. French chemist Antoine Lavoisier (1743–1794) placed sulfur among the unique substances that could not be separated, and called them "elements." Lavoisier's theory became accepted scientific fact in 1809, when chemists Joseph-Louis Gay-Lussac and Louis-Jacques Thénard proved Lavoisier correct. But what is an element? And what makes an element like sulfur so unique?

An element is a substance made up of only one kind of atom. Atoms are the basic building blocks of all the matter in the universe; they cannot be broken down into simpler substances. Pure sulfur is made up of only sulfur atoms. Similarly, pure carbon is made up entirely of carbon atoms.

Sulfur at a Glance

Chemical Symbol: S
Classification: Nonmetal
Properties: Pale yellow, odorless, brittle solid, insoluble in water
Group Number: 16
Period: 3
Series: Nonmetals
Discovered By: Antoine Lavoisier, c. 1770s
Atomic Number: 16
Atomic Weight: 32.06 atomic mass units (amu)
Phase at room temperature: Solid
Electrons: 16
Electrons per Shell: 2, 8, 6
Density at 68°F (20°C):
    (Orthorhombic Allotrope) 2.07 g/cm³
    (Monoclinic Allotrope) 1.96 g/cm³
Melting Point: 235°F (112.8°C)
Boiling Point: 832.3°F (444.6°C)
Commonly Found: Earth's crust, soil, sea water,
    the atmosphere, meteorites, volcanoes, hot springs, swamps, fossil fuels, other
    planets, and bound to other metals

Sulfur is number 16 on the periodic table of elements.

Scientists have discovered or created 118 different kinds of atoms, each of which represents a unique element. Atoms are distinguished from each other by their physical and chemical properties.

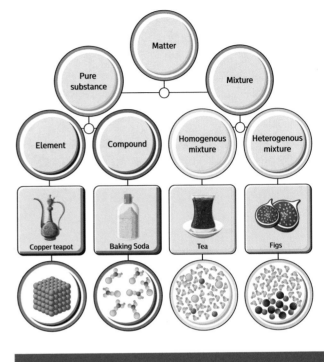

Elemental Recipes

Like individual ingredients in a recipe, elements combine with other elements to create the variety of substances all around you.

An element consists of one kind of atom, whereas a compound is made of two or more elements.

Specifically, atoms of the various elements combine to create molecules and compounds. Molecules contain at least two atoms, and compounds contain at least two *different kinds* of atoms. For example, two atoms of the element hydrogen (H) combine with one atom of the element oxygen (O) to create a molecule of water (H_2O).

Later, we will see how atoms of sulfur combine with atoms of other elements to make some useful compounds. First, let's look at the unique properties of sulfur itself.

2

Inside Sulfur

//

Sulfur is a solid at room temperature, because of the unique arrangement of sulfur atoms. Rather than existing alone or in pairs like many other types of nonmetal atoms, sulfur atoms naturally arrange themselves in crooked rings of eight sulfur atoms each.

These rings, or S_8 molecules, are often referred to as *crowns*, for reasons that are obvious from diagrams that illustrate the structure. Multiple S_8 crowns will naturally arrange themselves in organized crystal patterns. These distinct arrangements of S_8 molecules result in the allotropes, or different solid forms, of sulfur.

Sulfur Allotropes

The most common naturally occurring allotrope of elemental sulfur is called orthorhombic sulfur, a brittle yellow solid.

At temperatures above 204.8°F (96°C), another crystal arrangement forms. This one, known as monoclinic sulfur, is a paler yellow.

A third allotrope of sulfur, named amorphous, or plastic sulfur,
occurs when molten sulfur is cooled so quickly that its atoms do
not have time to arrange into S_8 crowns. Unless the atoms are
in S_8 crowns, orthorhombic or monoclinic crystal arrangements

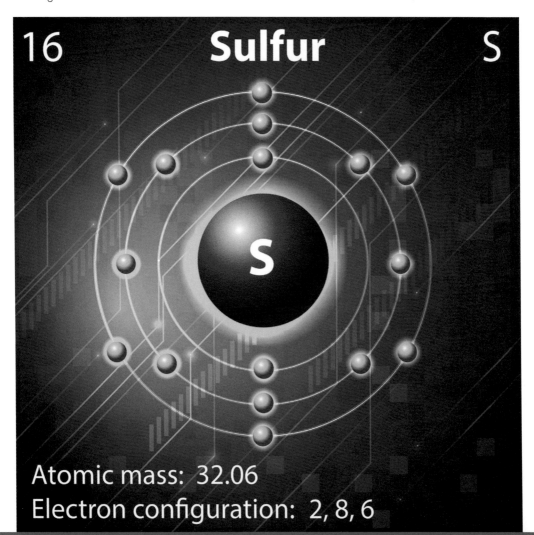

16   **Sulfur**   S

Atomic mass: 32.06
Electron configuration: 2, 8, 6

This Illustration shows the sixteen electrons that
circle around the nucleus of a sulfur atom. The
electrons are blue here, while the nucleus is red.

cannot form. Instead, the quickly cooled individual sulfur atoms form long chains that give plastic sulfur its characteristic softness and elasticity, or stretchiness.

Sulfur Breaks the Rules

The term *viscosity* refers to a substance's resistance to flow. Honey, for example, has a higher viscosity than water—try pouring honey and then water, and see which is easier.

Typically, when substances are melted, they become *less* viscous. In other words, as temperature rises, viscosity tends to decrease. If honey is heated, it is much easier to pour.

Sulfur does not play by these rules. Just above its melting point of 235°F (112.8°C), sulfur is a flowing, orange-brown liquid. As the temperature rises, though, the molten sulfur actually becomes *more viscous*. The reason for this is that heating the sulfur above the melting point causes the S_8 crowns to

Sulfur can be found as a solid but also in its molten state, especially in and around volcanoes.

break and the individual sulfur atoms to rearrange themselves into long chains called polymers. These long chains become tangled and make molten sulfur very resistant to flow. If the temperature increases beyond 320° F (160°C), these polymer chains, will also break apart, resulting in black, liquid sulfur.

Getting Smaller: Protons, Neutrons, Electrons

All atoms, including sulfur atoms, are made up of smaller, subatomic particles called protons, neutrons, and electrons. Sulfur, and only sulfur, has sixteen protons. The number of protons in an atom is also the atom's atomic number. Therefore, the atomic number of sulfur is 16. If an atom has an atomic number other than 16, it is not a sulfur atom.

Protons, which have a positive electrical charge, are found in an atom's center, or nucleus. Also contained within the nucleus are an atom's neutrons. Neutrons are neutral, without an electrical charge, so the nucleus of an atom is always positively charged.

Typically, sulfur has sixteen neutrons within its nucleus. Unlike the number of protons, which always remains the same, the number of neutrons can vary. Sulfur atoms can also have seventeen, eighteen, or twenty neutrons. These different types of atoms are known as isotopes of sulfur.

Sulfur has several isotopes, but only four are stable. Stable isotopes do not break down. Sulfur's unstable isotopes, on the other hand, will break down into other elements in order to regain stability—a property known as radioactivity.

Negatively charged electrons circulate around the positively charged nucleus in spaces called shells. Each shell can hold only a certain number of electrons, with additional electrons spilling over to the next available shell. The number of electrons in a neutral atom always matches the number of protons, or atomic number. Electrons play two very important roles. First, the negatively charged electrons are attracted to the positively charged protons in the nucleus. This attraction, known as electromagnetic force, is what holds the atom together. Because the number of electrons and protons is equal, the negative and positive charges cancel each other out. This leaves the atom with no overall charge. Second, an atom's electrons are central to its ability to bind to other atoms and to form compounds. Particularly important are the electrons in the outermost electron shell, known as valence electrons.

Reacting Electronically

An atom tends to lose, gain, or even share electrons in order to fill its outermost electron shell. When an atom's outermost electron shell is full, the atom is more stable and less reactive.

A typical sulfur atom has three electron shells; the first contains two electrons, the second contains eight electrons, and the third

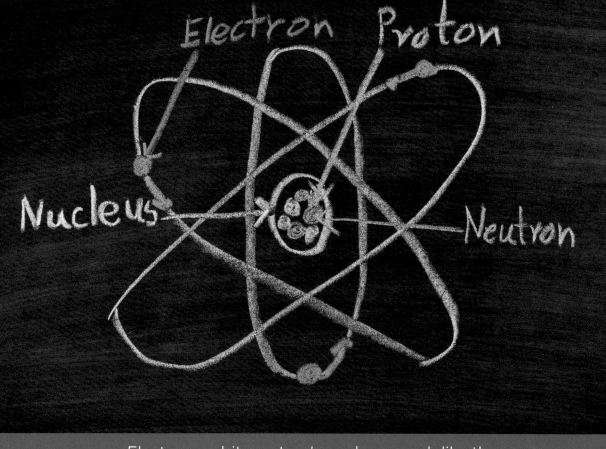

Electron   Proton

Nucleus

Neutron

Electrons orbit an atom's nucleus, much like the planets of solar systems orbit their stars. The nucleus contains an atom's protons and neutrons.

contains six electrons. This third electron shell is stable when it contains eight electrons. So, to attain stability, the sulfur atom will acquire two more electrons.

It can do so in two ways: it will either take two electrons from an atom that gives them up, or it will share two electrons with another atom. Taking electrons results in the formation of ions, producing an ionic bond. Sharing electrons with another atom does not produce ions and results instead in a covalent bond.

Sulfides, Sulfates, and Sulfites: The Differences

The sulfide ion, S^{2-}, is a sulfur atom that has gained two electrons. In addition to the sulfide ion, there are other common sulfur-containing ions. Some of them involve a sulfur atom, a particular number of oxygen atoms, and a negative two charge. There is the sulfate ion, SO_4^{2-}, which combines with other elements to form compounds collectively known as sulfates. A common sulfate is barium sulfate, $BaSO_4$.

Another common sulfur ion is the sulfite ion, SO_3^{2-}, which has one less oxygen atom than the sulfate ion. The sulfite ion combines with other elements to create compounds known as sulfites, such as sodium sulfite, Na_2SO_3. Sulfides, sulfates, and sulfites each have different chemical properties.

Bonding Ionically

When an atom gains electrons with a negative charge, the atom's electrons and protons no longer cancel out each other. Instead, for each electron an atom gains, its negative charge increases. Similarly, for each electron an atom loses, its positive charge increases. Charged atoms are called ions.

Two sodium (Na) atoms will each give up one electron to a single sulfur atom to form a compound made of two stable sodium ions with a positive one charge ($2Na^{1+}$) and one stable sulfur ion with a negative two charge (S^{2-}). These ions are stable because both the Na atoms and the S atom have now filled their outermost electron shells. Because the S^{2-} ion has a charge that is equal and opposite to the combined charge of the two Na^{1+} ions ($1^+ + 1^+ = 2^+$), all three ions "stick" together in a stable compound called a sulfide.

Covalent Bonding

In certain situations, atoms share electrons rather than accepting or giving them up entirely. The sharing of electrons between atoms is known as covalent bonding. Covalent bonding does not involve ions.

Sulfur, in addition to forming ionic bonds, is also capable of forming covalent bonds. Sulfur forms ionic bonds when it combines with metal atoms and covalent bonds when it combines with nonmetal atoms.

3

Sulfur's Place on the Periodic Table of Elements

//

Sulfur is one of 118 elements, 94 of which occur naturally. The others have been created in laboratories under conditions that don't normally occur. It is very possible that there are elements yet to be discovered. In 1869, Russian chemist Dmitry Mendeleev attempted to arrange the elements so his students could easily remember them.

First, Mendeleev arranged the elements in horizontal rows in order of increasing atomic weight. After arranging the known elements, he noted regular, repeating patterns of such properties as density, reactivity, and boiling points. These repeating patterns—or periods—led Mendeleev to call his construction the periodic table of elements.

Mendeleev's arrangement of the elements was not perfect, as there were gaps between elements. The ambitious chemist asserted that that the gaps in his table represented elements that had yet to be discovered. Based on the location of these gaps, Mendeleev even predicted the properties of the missing elements. Within twenty years of the first publication of Mendeleev's periodic table, three of these gaps were filled with newly discovered elements. Incredibly, the characteristics closely matched Mendeleev's predictions!

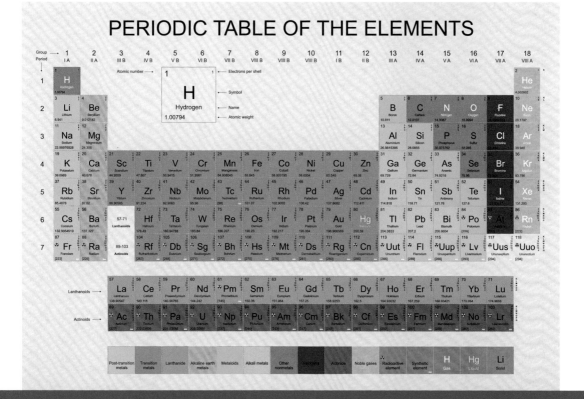

Mendeleev's periodic table of elements has been updated since he invented it in the 1800s, but the structure remains useful today.

A Stinky Substance?

Pure sulfur has no smell, but many sulfur compounds do. These compounds include chemicals known as thiols, mercaptans, and disulfides. Sulfur compounds are responsible for the pungent odors associated with skunks, matches, onions, garlic—and rotten eggs. They are also responsible for the stench of pollutants from some power plants and factories. Smelly mercaptans are purposefully added to natural gas to make leaks more easily detectable.

Pure sulfur has no smell, but sulfur compounds can smell terrible!

More than one hundred years have passed since the publication of the first periodic table of elements, and the table has undergone several changes, including the inclusion of more than fifty additional elements. Mendeleev's overall scheme still serves as its basis. Today, the elements are arranged in order of increasing atomic number, or number of protons, rather than atomic weight. They are arranged in horizontal rows, or periods, labeled one through seven. Moving from left to right across a period, each successive element has one more electron in its outer electron shell than the one before it. This leads to a predictable pattern of change in the physical and chemical behaviors of the elements.

The eighteen vertical columns of the periodic table are called groups, which are labeled IA through VIIA, IB through VIIIB, and 0. Elements in a group have the same number of electrons in their outer shells, resulting in some similar chemical behaviors. The elements of a given group are considered members of the same family.

Location, Location, Location

Sulfur is located in Period 3 and Group VIA (16) of the periodic table. All elements in group VIA have six electrons in their outer shells. This means that a sulfur atom gains two electrons from other

Sulfur is bright yellow and non-metallic, the tenth most common element in the universe by mass.

atoms to become stable. This strong tendency to gain electrons makes sulfur and the other Group VIA elements very reactive.

The number in the upper left-hand corner of sulfur's square represents the element's atomic number. Because all sulfur atoms have sixteen protons, sulfur's atomic number is sixteen. The number in the upper right-hand corner represents the element's atomic weight. This is the average relative mass of a sulfur atom, a measurement related to the number of protons plus the average number of neutrons in the atom. Electrons do not factor into an atom's atomic weight because they are so light.

Armed with some background information on sulfur, how it reacts with other atoms, and where it fits in relation to other elements, we can take a look at some of the important uses of sulfur and its compounds.

4

The Uses of Sulfur Compounds

///

Sulfur and sulfur compounds are used in the production of some medications, wine, gunpowder, matches, and artificial sweeteners. They are also used in pesticides and products that kill fungi, weeds, insects, and rodents. Sulfur is also present in grease- and oil-removing detergents, in some types of batteries, and in fertilizers. The element is also necessary for the vulcanization (hardening) of rubber and in some food preservation techniques.

One of sulfur's most important uses is in the manufacturing of sulfuric acid, a chemical with countless industrial roles. Despite their usefulness, sulfur compounds can be extremely dangerous, toxic, and harmful to the environment. For this reason, they must be handled with great care.

Sulfuric Acid

The primary use of sulfur is to manufacture sulfuric acid. Discovered by an eighth-century alchemist, this clear, odorless, extremely corrosive and oily acid was originally called oil of vitriol.

Mixing specific amounts of sulfuric acid with water can produce different concentrations of the acid and, therefore, different strengths. This process is called dilution. Different strengths of sulfuric acid have different uses. For example, 10 percent sulfuric

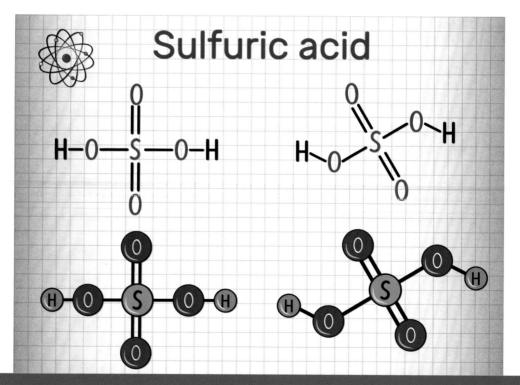

More sulfuric acid is produced annually than any other chemical; it is used in fertilizers, the production of dyes, and synthetic fabrics.

acid (90 percent water) is commonly used in laboratories, while car batteries typically use 35 percent sulfuric acid (65 percent water).

Mixing water and sulfuric acid releases enough heat to make the container hot to the touch. When water is poured into concentrated sulfuric acid, the water immediately begins to boil. For this reason, water is never added to sulfuric acid. Instead, the acid is added in small amounts to the water.

Given its industrial uses, more sulfuric acid is produced annually than any other chemical. Sulfuric acid is added to phosphate-containing rocks to produce phosphate fertilizers for crops and plants. It is also used to remove impurities from oil and mineral ores, in the creation of other important chemicals, and in waste-water processing.

Sulfuric acid is also involved in the production of certain paints and dyes, car batteries, and synthetic fibers like Rayon. It is also crucial in the "pickling" of iron and steel, a surface-cleaning process that prepares these metals for refining and coating, or plating, with other metals. The iron and steel are bathed in sulfuric acid, which dissolves impurities, such as oxidized iron scale, that build up on their surfaces.

Because it is highly reactive, sulfuric acid can be an extremely dangerous chemical. Even weak sulfuric acid is capable of dissolving many metals. A strip of zinc placed in a beaker of sulfuric acid will immediately begin bubbling and fizzing. In a short amount of time, no trace of the metal strip will remain. Sulfuric acid also reacts with human skin, pulling all of the water out of the skin cells and leaving behind an extremely painful acid burn. To protect themselves from accidental injury, scientists who work with sulfuric acid always wear protective goggles and clothing.

Sulfur Dioxide—SO_2

Sulfur dioxide is a colorless, poisonous gas used in the production of sulfuric acid and as a food preservative. As a preservative, sulfur dioxide is used in small quantities to deter the growth of mold and bacteria in various foods and beverages including raisins, dried apricots, and wine.

Sulfur dioxide is also used to give electrons to compounds in certain dyes and pigments, resulting in decolorization, or bleaching. This property of sulfur dioxide makes the compound useful in the production of some fabrics and papers. Over time, oxygen in the air takes the donated electrons back from the bleached

Sulfur dioxide is a harmful byproduct of many industrial and power-generating processes, particularly the combustion, or burning, of coal and petroleum.

pigments in a process called oxidation. As a result of oxidation, bleached items regain some color. For example, bleached newspaper will eventually return to its original yellow color.

Although useful, sulfur dioxide is also problematic. It is a harmful byproduct of many industrial and power generating processes, particularly the combustion, or burning, of coal and petroleum. Sulfur dioxide is also emitted naturally by volcanoes and certain microorganisms, though in less dangerous amounts.

Acid Rain

Each year, millions of tons of sulfur dioxide (SO_2) are released from smokestacks of coal-burning power plants. When sulfur dioxide is released into the air, it reacts with oxygen to create sulfur trioxide, or SO_3. When SO_3 mixes with water droplets in the air, sulfuric acid is produced. Sulfur dioxide can also

Producing Energy and Sulfur

Many power plants in the United States and other countries burn coal to generate electricity. Because coal contains sulfur, these power plants are an enormous source of poisonous, acid rain-producing sulfur dioxide. To help manage this problem, scientists are seeking ways to reduce sulfur dioxide gas emissions. One approach is to burn only low-sulfur coals.

In addition, the Environmental Protection Agency requires many coal-fired plants to use special apparatuses called scrubbers. These are built into smokestacks to remove much of the sulfur dioxide from the smoke before it is released to the air. Other fuels, including some types of coal, are desulfurized using chemicals to bind and remove the sulfur they contain.

mix directly with water droplets in the air to produce a weaker acid called sulfurous acid. Both of these acids then fall to the earth as acid rain.

Acid rain is costly to the environment. It damages trees at high altitudes and raises the acidity of lakes, streams, and soils, disrupting the ecological balance needed to sustain many plants and animals. Acid rain can destroy the façades of historical buildings and statues by causing them to break down faster. Common building materials are eroded by acid rain, including limestone, sandstone, and some metals and paints.

Hydrogen Sulfide—H_2S

Hydrogen sulfide is a foul smelling, flammable, poisonous gas that results from the decay, or breakdown, of organic matter. It is the smell of rotten eggs, and is also emitted from volcanoes and hot springs. It is a component of natural gas. The powerful odor sometimes present near swamps or sewers is due to hydrogen sulfide gas. Many bacteria in these low-oxygen environments consume sulfur-containing substances in order to produce energy, and hydrogen sulfide gas is released as a byproduct of this process. The hydrogen sulfide released by bacteria in the human digestive tract and mouth is, in part, responsible for the odors associated with flatulence and bad breath!

Inhaling hydrogen sulfide gas is potentially deadly. The poisonous gas affects many systems in the body, most notably the nervous

Metal sulfides are compounds that contain sulfur and one or more metals. Shown here are realgar (yellow), stibnite (grey), galena, and pyrite.

system. Despite its toxicity, hydrogen sulfide gas has found some use in industry, particularly in the formation of other important sulfur compounds, the metal sulfides.

Metal Sulfides

Metal sulfides are compounds that contain sulfur and one or more metals. For example, the combination of lead (Pb) and sulfur results in lead sulfide, or PbS. One of the better known metal sulfides is pyrite, an iron sulfide (FeS_2) nicknamed "fool's gold" due its striking resemblance to real gold ore. Many of the metal sulfides occur naturally in minerals; others are made in laboratories using the sulfur from hydrogen sulfide gas.

Sulfates

Sulfates are compounds that contain sulfur and oxygen in the form of the sulfate ion, SO_4^{2-}. The sulfate ion can ionically bond to many metal ions. Zinc sulfate ($ZnSO_4$) is a common metal sulfate. Sodium sulfate (Na_2SO_4) is a common filler in laundry detergents. Such fillers do not actually act as the cleaning agent, but enhance the detergent's cleaning action. Sodium sulfate is also used in the textile, paper processing, and glass industries.

Copper sulfate ($CuSO_4$) is a bright blue salt that can be used in hair dyes, as a fungicide, and in leather processing. Other metal sulfates are used as catalysts to speed up chemical reactions. Potassium aluminum sulfate ($KAlSO_4$), also called alum, is used in packaging some foods, notably pickles.

5

Everyday Sulfur

Sulfur's unique atomic structure gives the element an astonishingly wide array of applications in fields from warfare to medicine.

Strengthening Rubber

Rubber is used to make a variety of items, from waterproof raincoats to tire treads, pencil erasers to elastic bands. Natural rubber is made from latex, a substance in the sap of rubber trees. Latex is a polymer called polyisoprene, which is made up of many smaller molecules joined together in a long chain. The random polymer structure of latex gives rubber some remarkable qualities. For example, it is elastic (it can be stretched repeatedly beyond its original length), and it is largely resistant to water, temperature changes, and many chemicals.

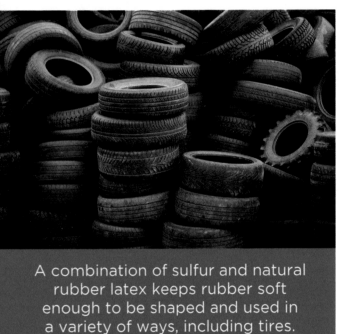

A combination of sulfur and natural rubber latex keeps rubber soft enough to be shaped and used in a variety of ways, including tires.

In the 1830s, Charles Goodyear discovered that heating a mixture of natural latex and sulfur turned soft, pliable, rubber into a much harder substance with broader applications. The process, called vulcanization—after Vulcan, the Roman god of fire—is still used today.

How does vulcanization work? When sulfur and latex are mixed and heated, the S_8 crowns bond to the latex polymers, creating cross-links between them. The sulfur cross-links anchor the polymers in place and make it harder for the formerly free-moving chains to move around. This makes vulcanized rubber much more heat resistant and less likely to wear down. Vulcanized rubber is crucial to the production of car and truck tires, boots, hoses, brake and engine parts, and even hockey pucks.

Warfare

Warriors of the Byzantine Empire hurled Greek fire at their enemies. This fiery liquid, which contained elemental sulfur, was especially useful when fighting naval battles, as it would stick to anything it touched and continued to burn when floating on water.

Using elemental sulfur as a principal ingredient, the Chinese invented gunpowder, the first explosive, around the tenth century. The recipe spread quickly to Europe and beyond. Today, sulfur-containing gunpowder, a low-level explosive, is still used in fireworks and signal flares. A sulfur compound was also a component of mustard gas, a controversial and highly toxic weapon used during World War I to inflict painful skin and lung blistering, blindness, and frequently, death.

A Dietary Element

The same element that hardens rubber, contributes to acid rain formation, and is part of very toxic gases is also required for life. Without sulfur, all microorganisms, plants and animals would die.

The Sulfur Cycle

Sulfur is constantly passed back and forth through soil, the atmosphere, and the oceans in a complex process known as the sulfur cycle. Plants, animals, and bacteria each play an important part in this cycle by absorbing sulfur in different forms and releasing it for the next phase of the cycle.

Animals eat plants that contain sulfur compounds. When the animals die, bacteria consume their flesh, turning the bodies' organic sulfur into inorganic sulfides, sulfites, and eventually sulfates. Plants absorb these inorganic sulfur compounds to produce organic sulfur compounds that animals will once again eat.

Much like the carbon cycle, the sulfur cycle is an ongoing process on our planet, where sulfur leaches from one item to another—getting into the soil, the water, the air.

Sulfur is found in every cell in our bodies. Without it, cellular respiration, the process by which our cells create energy, would shut down. Sulfur is part of essential amino acids, the building blocks of proteins that are crucial to the cellular structures and functions that sustain life.

One of these essential amino acids is methionine. In our bodies, methionine turns into another sulfur-containing amino acid called cysteine. The sulfur in cysteine molecules plays a crucial role in folding proteins into their correct shapes. The sulfur atoms in cysteine molecules form bridges, or cross-links between two sulfur atoms, that help proteins keep their shape. Without these sulfur bridges, the function of many proteins would be disrupted. Examples of these sulfur-dependent proteins are keratin (part of hair, skin, and nails) and collagen (part of connective tissue like cartilage).

Where do we get the elemental sulfur we need to make proteins? Plants have the ability to take sulfur in ionic form (inorganic) and break it down to sulfur in molecular (organic) form. Unlike plants, animals—including humans—cannot do this. Neither can we produce our own methionine. We must rely on the foods we eat to provide us with essential amino acids. Foods rich in methionine include fruits, meats, fish, nuts, soy, mushrooms, potatoes, some beans, and such vegetables as spinach, peas, corn, cauliflower, avocados, sprouts, and broccoli. Dietary sulfur is also present in milk, onions, garlic, cabbage, turnips, and Brussels sprouts. By eating a normal, healthy diet, humans get plenty of dietary sulfur.

INFOGRAPHIC
SULFUR. FOOD SOURCES

Sulfur is an essential component of all living cells.
For example, the high strength of hair, skin and nails is due in part to the high content of sulfur. In intracellular chemistry, sulfur acts as a carrier of reducing hydrogen and its electrons for cellular repair of oxidation.

Crystal lattice

BASICS OF HEALTHY NUTRITION

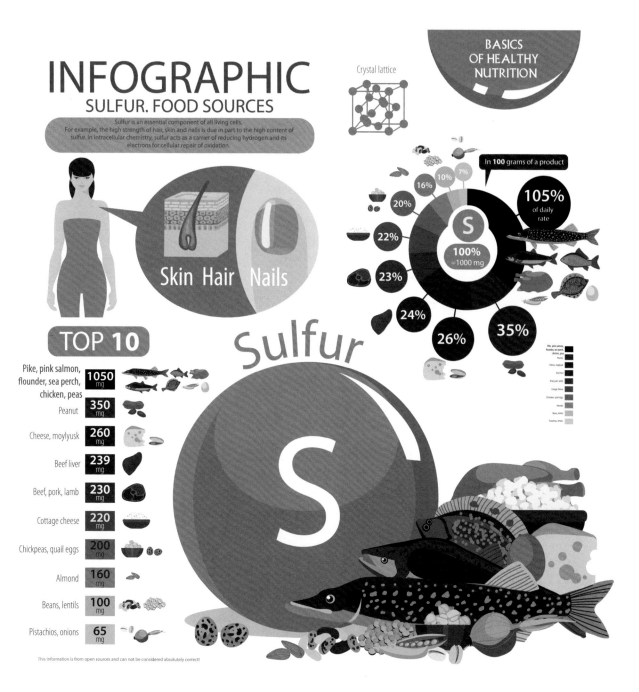

Skin Hair Nails

In **100** grams of a product

S

100%
=1000 mg

105%
of daily rate

16% 10% 7%
20%
22%
23%
24%
26% 35%

Sulfur

TOP 10

Food	Amount
Pike, pink salmon, flounder, sea perch, chicken, peas	1050 mg
Peanut	350 mg
Cheese, moylyusk	260 mg
Beef liver	239 mg
Beef, pork, lamb	230 mg
Cottage cheese	220 mg
Chickpeas, quail eggs	200 mg
Almond	160 mg
Beans, lentils	100 mg
Pistachios, onions	65 mg

This information is from open sources and can not be considered absolutely correct!

Are you surprised to know that you've probably eaten sulfur? Fish, cheese, and eggs all contain this element.

Thiamine (vitamin B$_1$) is a sulfur-containing vitamin that helps the body convert carbohydrates and fat into energy. It is present in foods such as tuna, sunflower seeds, many cereals, and beans. Thiamine is necessary for normal growth and development and helps to maintain proper function of the heart and the nervous and digestive systems. Biotin (vitamin B$_7$), another vitamin crucial to energy production, also contains sulfur.

Medical Applications

Sulfur was used in prehistoric times to ease stomach upset. Sometimes sulfur was mixed with wool fat (lanolin) to treat skin infections.

In the early twentieth century, substances used in dyes were found to fight bacterial infections. While sulfa drugs are still used today, many have been replaced with members of another sulfur-containing class of antibiotics known as penicillins.

Dermatologists prescribe sulfur-based creams and ointments to treat acne, skin inflammation, and scabies—a parasitic infection. Some sulfates are used for medicinal purposes. Magnesium sulfate (MgSO$_4$), commonly called Epsom salts, is sometimes used to slow labor contractions in pregnant women. Barium sulfate (BaSO$_4$) allows patients to safely swallow barium so that x-ray images can be taken of the digestive tract to look for abnormalities. Barium is normally toxic to humans, but the body cannot absorb the sulfate portions of the compound, so it is safe to use. The large nuclei of the barium atoms easily absorb X-rays to create clear images on X-ray film.

6

Naturally Occurring Sulfur

Sulfur is a major component of soil, and small amounts are also found in seawater and in the earth's atmosphere. Scientists believe that about 5 percent of the earth's core is made up of sulfur.

Volcanic Sulfur

Sulfur occurs naturally near volcanoes. Hydrogen sulfide gas bubbles up through cracks in the earth called fumaroles, while oxygen in the air transforms the gas back to elemental sulfur, leaving piles of the yellow stuff around the fumarole.

Through the 1800s, the biggest supply of sulfur in the world came from sulfur mines on the island of Sicily, home to the volcano Mount Etna. The sulfur-containing rocks collected from the mines were

Sulfur occurs in nature in and around volcanoes; volcanoes often steam with hydrogen sulfide gas.

spread on top of slabs and set on fire. The melted liquid sulfur ran out the sides, where it was collected. This was a rather inefficient process, as more than half the sulfur was wasted.

Today, similar volcanic sulfur deposits in Indonesia, Chile, and Japan still serve as good sources of sulfur.

Underground Sulfur

In the 1860s, speculators searching for oil stumbled across large underground deposits of relatively pure sulfur in Texas and Louisiana.

It was impossible with the technology of the times to affordably retrieve this high-quality sulfur.

In the 1890s, chemist Herman Frasch realized that the sulfur could be melted and pumped to the surface as a liquid. Frasch developed a process that pumped superheated steam and compressed air into the sulfur-filled underground caverns. The superheated steam melted the sulfur, and the compressed air forced the liquid sulfur to the surface. This technique, aptly named the Frasch Process, is still used today.

Metal-bound Sulfur

While sulfur does occur in its pure elemental form, it is often bound to metals like iron. In some places, iron sulfides are still the primary source of sulfur. Other metal sulfides from which pure sulfur can

Extraterrestrial Sulfur

Sulfur has been found in meteorites, on Mars, and on our moon. One of the more notable sulfur-rich places in our solar system is Io, one of Jupiter's moons. Io has more than four hundred volcanoes, which continuously throw sulfur into the air and onto the moon's surface. Io is so cold, sulfur dioxide-frost will often form.

Bacterial life has been found in extremely sulfur-rich environments on the earth, such as deep-sea hydrothermal vents. For this reason, some scientists theorize that Io, too, may be home to sulfur-using bacteria!

Jupiter's moon Io is a huge source of sulfur in our solar system—not that we can mine it there yet! Io contains hundreds of active volcanoes.

Piles of yellow sulfur await their final destinations at a sulfur factory. Sulfur has a wide array of applications in fields from warfare to medicine.

be extracted are mercury sulfide (cinnabar), lead sulfide (galena), and zinc sulfide (sphalerite). Sulfur is also found in oxygen-containing sulfate minerals including the calcium sulfates called anhydrite and gypsum.

Sulfur Gases

Fuel standards designed to protect the environment from harmful sulfur gases require that sulfur be removed from coal and natural gas. The reclaimed sulfur can be put to use in one of many sulfur-dependent industrial processes. The hydrogen sulfide gas removed from natural gases is a tremendous source of sulfur. The natural gas is sprayed with a special chemical that causes the hydrogen sulfide to dissolve. The isolated hydrogen sulfide is then combined with oxygen to produce water and pure sulfur.

Using scrubbers, as much as 95 percent of sulfur can be reclaimed from the sulfur dioxide gas emitted by coal-fired power plants and industrial plants. Scrubbers are required for newly built power plants, but environmental laws allow many older power facilities to operate without them.

Sulfur Summarized

We've explored nearly every facet of sulfur, from its discovery on earth to its existence in outer space. What will the future bring for sulfur?

In 2013, scientists at the University of Arizona began working on ways to turn sulfur waste into plastic. They found that by combining sulfur with DIB (1, 3-diisopropylbenzene) the sulfur polymers stabilize and no longer fall apart at high temperatures. The resulting plastic is simple to make and low-cost, making it attractive for all kinds of industries. This, along with continuing research, will keep sulfur part of American industry for a long time to come.

Glossary

allotropes Versions of the same element that have different chemical and physical properties.

atom Tiny particle from which all substances are made. With the exception of hydrogen, which has no neutrons, all stable atoms are made up of protons, neutrons, and electrons.

covalent bond Bond between two or more atoms that results from the sharing of electrons.

electromagnetic force Attractive force between objects with opposite charges (e.g., electrons and protons).

electron Negatively charged particle circulating around the nucleus of an atom.

electron shells Sphere-like spaces in which electrons circulate around the nucleus of an atom.

monoclinic One of the common crystalline structures into which sulfur atoms naturally arrange themselves.

orthorhombic Most common crystalline structure into which sulfur atoms naturally arrange themselves.

polymer Large molecule formed by the combination of several smaller similar molecules, called monomers.

proton Subatomic particle with a positive charge found in the nucleus of an atom.

radioactivity Spontaneous degradation of an element that emits radiation in the form of charged particles in order to reach a stable state.

subatomic particles Particles—including protons, neutrons, and electrons—that comprise atoms.

sulfates Chemical derivatives of sulfuric acid.

valence electrons Electrons traveling in the outermost electron shell of an atom.

vulcanization Process that involves heating rubber and sulfur together in order to harden the rubber.

Further Reading

Books

Adam, Nuhh. *Chemistry for Beginners: The 30 Most Astonishing Elements Around Us.* Amazon Digital Services, 2015.

Heinecke, Liz Lee. *Kitchen Science Lab for Kids.* Beverly, MA: Quarry Books, 2014.

Robinson, E. M. *Amber's Atoms: The First 10 Elements of the Periodic Table.* Design Friendly Press, 2016.

Slingerland, Janet. *Explore Atoms and Molecules!: With 25 Great Projects.* Amazon Digital Services, 2017.

Websites

Geology.com

geology.com/minerals/sulfur.shtml

Facts and photos about sulfur

Jefferson Lab

education.jlab.org/itselemental/ele016.html

Quick facts about sulfur

Live Science

www.livescience.com/28939-sulfur.html

The facts and latest news about sulfur

Bibliography

Atkins, P. W. *The Periodic Kingdom: A Journey into the Land of the Chemical Elements*. New York, NY: Basic Books, 1997.

Bauman, Robert. *Microbiology*. Second edition. San Francisco, CA: Pearson Benjamin Cummings, 2007.

Beatty, Richard. *Sulfur*. New York, NY: Benchmark Books, 2005.

Chang, Raymond. *Chemistry,* Eighth ed. New York, NY: McGraw-Hill, 2005.

Chung, Woo Jin, et al. "The Use of Elemental Sulfur as an Alternative Feedstock for Polymeric Materials." *Nature Chemistry* 5, 518–524 (2013), https://www.nature.com/articles/nchem.1624.

Emsley, John. *Nature's Building Blocks: An A–Z Guide to the Elements*. New York, NY: Oxford University Press, 2002.

Heiserman, David L. *Exploring Chemical Elements and Their Compounds*. New York, NY: McGraw-Hill, 1991.

Rogers, Kirsteen, et al. *The Usborne Internet-Linked Science Encyclopedia*. London, UK: Usborne Publishing Ltd., 2003.

Schenk, J. "Some Properties of Liquid Sulfur and the Occurrence of Long Chain Molecule." *Physica*, Volume 23, 1957.

Index